Citizen Scientists

Be a Part of Scientific Discovery from Your Own Backyard

Loree Griffin Burns

Photographs by **Ellen Harasimowicz**

Henry Holt and Company

NEW YORK

To Sam and Ben and Cat, cherished field companions,

and to Gerry, who supports us in every way

—L. G. B.

To my mother, Ethel Page, for everything

—E. H.

H SQUARE FISH

Imprints of Macmillan
175 Fifth Avenue, New York, New York 10010
mackids.com

Printed in China by RR Donnelley Asia Printing Solutions Ltd., Dongguan City, Guangdong Province.

Henry Holt® is a registered trademark of Henry Holt and Company, LLC. *Publishers since 1866.*
Square Fish and the Square Fish logo are trademarks of Macmillan and are used by Henry Holt and Company under license from Macmillan.

Library of Congress Cataloging-in-Publication Data
Burns, Loree Griffin.
Citizen scientists : be a part of scientific discovery from your own backyard / Loree Griffin Burns ; photographs by Ellen Harasimowicz.
p. cm.
Includes bibliographical references and index.
1. Suburban animals—Research—Citizen participation—Juvenile literature. 2. Suburban animals—Monitoring
—Citizen participation—Juvenile literature. I. Harasimowicz, Ellen, ill. II. Title.
QL51.B87 2012 590.72'3—dc23 2011031673

Originally published in the United States by Henry Holt and Company.
First Square Fish Edition: 2013
Designed by April Ward
Square Fish logo designed by Filomena Tuosto

ISBN 978-0-8050-9062-8 (Henry Holt hardcover)
3 5 7 9 10 8 6 4

ISBN 978-0-8050-9517-3 (Square Fish paperback)
5 7 9 10 8 6

AR: 6.8

CONTENTS

A monarch chrysalis
hangs from the leaf of
a milkweed plant.

What Is Citizen Science, Anyway?

It's not a phrase you hear every day, and it doesn't exactly roll off the tongue. But citizen science is the beating heart of this book, so we'd better start by defining it.

A **citizen** is any resident of our world. I'm a citizen, and so are you.

Science is a systematic study of our world, a way of understanding it by watching it closely, puzzling out how parts of it work, testing these ideas with experiments, and then sharing what we learn with the rest of humankind.

Citizen science, then, is the study of our world by the people who live in it. Not just professional people—scientists with degrees and laboratories and fancy equipment—but everyday people, too. All men, women, and children who use their senses and smarts to understand the world around them can be *citizen scientists*. And I happen to think YOU would be a great one. Why? Well, let me tell you a story. . . .

One day, while I was in the middle of writing this book, my daughter and I took a walk through a milkweed meadow. It was nearly October, and the sun was setting, which meant conditions weren't great for spotting a monarch butterfly chrysalis, but that is exactly what my daughter wanted to do. I suggested we look for ladybugs or caterpillars instead, but she would not be swayed.

"A chrysalis is pretty hard to find," I warned her. "I know adults who have searched for years and never found one."

She was walking behind me at this point, and I heard her laugh.

"It's really not that hard, Mom," she said.

I turned to disagree, to tell her about the man I'd read about who had been watching and raising monarch butterflies for more than 20 years and had never, not once, seen a chrysalis in the wild. And there was my daughter, nose to pupa with a chrysalis, right there in *our* wild. She was studying the golden threads, the droplets of dew, the silken pad holding the whole thing up.

I realized in that moment something I had known all along but had yet to write down in my book: Young people see the world differently than older people do. And when it comes to working in the field as a citizen scientist, these differences are important.

For example, think about size. My daughter is only four feet tall, which means that chrysalis she found was practically at eye level. I'm five feet seven inches tall, and the chrysalis was so far under my nose I didn't even notice it. As a kid, you're closer to the world under your feet than you will ever be again. This can be an advantage in the field.

There is also the issue of sensitivity. At 40 years old, I don't perceive sights, sounds, smells, touches, and tastes as well as I once did. My daughter's senses, on the other hand, are still developing. Each day she sees and hears and smells and feels and tastes a little better than the day before. She's only just coming into her prime as an observer of the world—and the same is true for you.

Finally, let's talk about focus. As I walked

with my daughter that day, my eyes were on the meadow around me, but my mind was in lots of places. I was thinking about finding a chrysalis, of course, but also about a whole list of other things: my daughter and how nice it was to spend time with her; what I would make for dinner that night; how I needed to remember to stop and buy a gallon of milk on the way home; how well (or not) I had written about this magical place—the milkweed meadow—in my work that morning. I was living in several moments at once; my daughter was focused on the one and only moment at hand. And so *she* found something extraordinary.

Living close to the earth, being observant, and staying focused are excellent traits for a scientist to have. And kids—kids like you—come by these traits naturally. I hope this book will inspire you to embrace them and to begin your work as a citizen scientist. And I hope you'll share the extraordinary things you find with the rest of us!

One last thing: Please don't worry if you don't happen to live near a milkweed meadow. Many of us don't. The exciting truth is that we need to understand wildlife in all sorts of settings, from rural country fields to busy urban parks. The number and type of wildlife you will observe in each location are very different, and there are particular citizen science projects that will be better suited to each, but the bottom line is that what you observe where you live—no matter where that is—is important. Whether you are in your backyard or in the park near your friend's house or watching the window box outside your high-rise apartment, there are things to see. Keep your senses open to the sights and sounds of your little patch of the world, record what you experience, then look at the back of this book for a list of several organizations that may be interested in knowing what you have discovered.

Loree Burns

The monarch butterfly's bright orange and black markings are easy to recognize in the field, as is the mitten-shaped discal cell.

CHAPTER ONE
FALL BUTTERFLYING

Butterfly eyes can detect movement, so when you sneak up on your monarch, net raised high over your head, be sure to move slowly. Do not point. Do not let your shadow fall on the butterfly. Breathe quietly.

If something does startle your butterfly into flight, don't panic. It will land again. Be patient. Watch closely. Keep your net ready.

When the butterfly lands again, creep toward it. Slowly. Quietly. When you are near enough, inch the opening of your net alongside its perch. Take a deep breath.

Are you ready?

SWING!

If the swing was a good one, the butterfly will now be in the tapered end of your net. Wrap your free hand around a wider part of the net—above the butterfly—so that it can't escape. Take another deep breath.

You did it! You captured a monarch butterfly!

Although temporarily a prisoner, your monarch is just fine. The mesh of your net is soft, and the body of a butterfly is hardier than it looks.

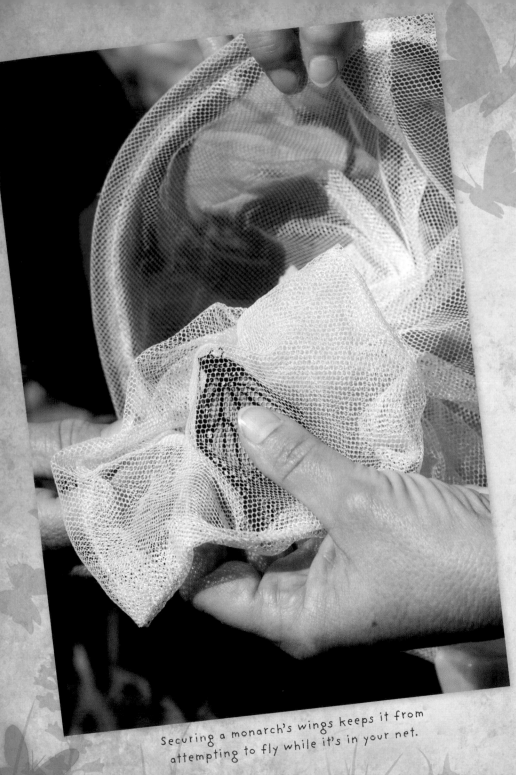

Securing a monarch's wings keeps it from attempting to fly while it's in your net.

This one will soon be fluttering about the meadow again. Before that can happen, though, you've got to tag it.

Find a comfortable spot in the meadow, preferably somewhere you can kneel down. Be sure to keep the net closed as you move. When you're ready, grab the butterfly's wings—all four of them—between your thumb and forefinger, right through the net. Now slide your free hand into the net and, once again, grab the butterfly's wings between your forefinger and thumb. Once you've got hold of the butterfly with your bare hand, you can let go with the hand holding on through the net.

Gently—*very* gently—pull the butterfly out. You may feel some resistance; butterflies have hooks on their feet that can snag on the mesh of the net. If you pull too quickly or with too much force, you can actually tear the butterfly's leg off. Do not rush. Work slowly.

When the butterfly is out, look it over. Observe the jet black eyes, clubbed antennae, jointed legs, and chunky abdomen. Admire the thousands of colored scales that make the wings look like stained glass windows: panes of brilliant orange divided by silky black veins. Note the splotches of white dotting the black edges of each wing and spilling over to decorate the head and upper body, too. These markings will help you verify the butterfly you have caught is actually a monarch.

Please don't worry if what you've caught is not a monarch at all, but a look-alike butterfly. It happens. Study the impostor, make note of its markings so that you can correctly identify it later, and when you are ready, let it go. No harm done.

If your butterfly is indeed a monarch, sex it. That is, figure out whether you have captured a male or a female. To do this, you'll have to look at the upper surfaces of the hind wings. This will require nimble hands. Keep hold of the four wings with one hand, and with your free fingers, gently tease apart the hind wings so that you can peek at their upper sides. You should see a black and orange pattern identical to the one on the underside of the wings. If your butterfly is a male, you will also see two black bulges along the wing veins, one near the center of each hind

Male monarch butterflies (top) have scent pouches on the upper side of their hind wings; females (bottom) do not. In some males you can see evidence of these pouches even on the underside of the wing.

wing. These are scent pouches, and only male monarchs have them.

Now you are ready for the main event: tagging your butterfly. This, too, requires nimble hands. Better yet, an assistant. Looking at the underside

11

Butterfly tags can be hard for adult hands to manipulate—yet another advantage for the young citizen scientist.

Tags do not appear to hurt the butterfly or to affect its ability to fly.

Getting an up-close look at the regal monarch is the prize of a day spent tagging.

of the hind wing—the surface your thumb and forefinger are touching—locate the largest orange area, the mitten-shaped window known as the discal cell. Place your tag gently over that cell. Once the tag is in place, press your thumb over it firmly to make sure it is stuck.

There. You're done. Your monarch is tagged.

Open your free hand and place the monarch's feet onto your palm. Slowly let go of its wings. Your monarch may stay in your palm for a while, adjusting to the tag and to its freedom. It may open and close its wings or run its proboscis over your palm. Very few people have experienced this particular tickle; savor it!

Watch your monarch for as long as it lets you. Ask your assistant to take a photo or two. When your monarch lifts off, watch it go. Wish it well. Then pick up your net, gather your assistant, and turn your attention back to the meadow. Scan the horizon for another flurry of orange and black.

Do you see one?

Great.

Go get it!

oluteers have been tagging monarch butterflies since 1952, when Dr. Fred Urquhart first invited the general public to help him track the species. At that time, scientists knew only that monarchs didn't spend the winter in the same regions of eastern North America where they spent their summers. Instead, monarchs headed south, presumably in search of warmer weather. Exactly where they went, or what they did when they got there, was a mystery.

Dr. Urquhart thought he might be able to solve this mystery by marking monarchs in some way. If he marked a monarch in Toronto, for example, and released it, perhaps someone who happened to live along the path this monarch flew might notice it and let Urquhart know. This information would tell him the direction the butterfly was headed and how long it had taken to get there. If he marked and released enough monarchs, and heard back from enough people, Urquhart thought he might be able to figure out where the monarchs were going.

Urquhart tags were rectangular; this one was returned to scientists in Mexico in 2009.

So, Dr. Urquhart and his wife, Norah, developed tags that were stamped with unique serial numbers and the message "Report No. [number] to Zoology University Toronto Canada," and they stuck them onto the wings of monarch butterflies. By 1971, the Urquharts had recruited 600 men, women, and children to help them with the tagging program. The Urquharts analyzed the movement of thousands of monarchs, and eventually a pattern emerged: Monarchs tagged east of the Rocky Mountains always flew toward Mexico.

Hundreds of thousands of tags and several years later, Dr. Urquhart made a thrilling discovery. In early January 1975, high in the mountains of central Mexico, Urquhart's colleagues—with the help of local residents—located a forest of fir trees covered with monarch butterflies. As Urquhart later wrote, the monarchs "clung in tightly packed masses to every branch and trunk of the tall, gray-green oyamel trees. They swirled through the air like autumn leaves and carpeted the ground in their flaming myriads." Among these myriads were butterflies with wings bearing the Urquhart tag; a winter colony of eastern monarch butterflies had been found at last! Urquhart and his team eventually found several mountaintop forests, all within a small area of Mexico, where huge populations of monarch butterflies gathered for the winter.

The first report of Urquhart's success was printed in the August 1976 issue of *National Geographic* magazine.

It's astonishing, really. Insects that are at most four inches from wingtip to wingtip, that each weigh less than a single peanut, somehow make their way from as far north as Canada to a handful of mountaintop forests in central Mexico. That's a flight of more than 2,000 miles in some cases, and it is accomplished on wings as thin as paper. As if this weren't intriguing enough, there's this: Not a single one of these butterflies has ever been to Mexico before.

Here's how it seems to work, at least for most monarch butterflies. Summertime monarchs emerge and for two weeks live the life of a typical butterfly: They mate and, if they are female, lay eggs. These monarchs are called the breeding generation. The caterpillars that hatch from their eggs grow, molt, and pupate over a four-week period, eventually transforming into adult butterflies themselves. If it is still high summer when these new adult butterflies emerge—that is,

Monarch butterflies glow against Mexico's bright February skies.

Several monarch overwintering sites in Mexico's Transvolcanic Mountains have been turned into government-protected butterfly sanctuaries that attract thousands of local and international tourists every year. This photograph was taken at Cerro Pelón in February 2009.

if nights are warm and days arc long—they, too, will mate, becoming a second breeding generation. If, however, adult monarch butterflies emerge at the end of summer—when days are shorter and nights are colder—their lives unfold very differently. Instead of mating, these butterflies become the migrating generation of monarchs. They feed heavily on nectar from late-blooming plants and, eventually, fly toward Mexico. Although many die on the way, most will reach the Mexican wintering grounds.

Unlike their short-lived breeding-generation cousins, migrating monarchs can live as long as nine months. The bulk of this time is spent hanging motionless from fir trees at the Mexican wintering sites. The climate in these mountaintop forests is unique: cold enough to push the butterflies into a hibernation-like state, moist enough to keep them from dehydrating, but not so cold and moist that the butterflies freeze.

In spring, when temperatures on the mountains rise, the butterflies shake off the sluggishness of winter. A frenzy of spring activity begins, and the monarchs—millions and millions of them—eat and drink and mate. They migrate again, this time flying north. Most succumb to old age and the elements before they get very far, but many

Thousands of monarch butterflies clustered in the branches of a tree at one of the Mexican overwintering sites.

live long enough to produce a new generation of monarch eggs. These eggs develop into the first breeding generation of the new summer season, mating and continuing the journey north. By the end of summer, monarchs will

A mating pair of migrating monarch butterflies. Notice how faded their colors are after a long migration and an even longer winter in Mexico.

have repopulated their entire summertime range, from Texas to southern Canada.

How do the butterflies find the same wintering sites year after year?

Why do butterflies that emerge in the fall behave so differently from butterflies that emerge in the summer?

What signals the migrating butterflies to begin their journey, and what signals them to reverse it in the spring?

How many of the butterflies survive the journey?

What happens to those that don't?

How do weather and environmental conditions affect the migration?

Scientists are still studying these and many other questions about the monarch migration. Dr. Orley "Chip" Taylor, a professor at the University of Kansas, is confident that tagging more monarchs will reveal important answers. When Fred and Norah Urquhart retired, Chip founded Monarch Watch to continue their tagging program. The organization is dedicated to understanding and preserving the

Chip collects recovered tags from Mexicans living near one of the overwintering sites.

monarch migration through tagging and educational programs.

"If you are interested in conserving a particular organism, you have to understand it," says Chip. "You really have to understand every little aspect of its biology."

And so he oversees the printing, distribution, and recovery of thousands of butterfly tags each year. Chip estimates that more than 100,000 people participate in Monarch Watch's annual tagging programs, many of them through their classrooms or local nature centers.

"We are learning something new every year," Chip says. "And we've learned a lot of things from the tagging that I didn't anticipate."

One thing Chip learned is that mortality—that is, the chance that a butterfly will die on the journey to Mexico—is closely tied to where the butterfly begins its migration. Butterflies tagged in Kansas, for example, seem to complete the journey to Mexico much more often than butterflies tagged in Massachusetts.

All of which raises the question: Where do you live?

If you live in New England, you will have to tag a lot of monarchs before one of your tags is recovered in Mexico. On the other hand, if you live in the Midwest, chances are better that one of your tags will one day be returned to Chip. Either way, your tagging work will put you in a small but important group of North American citizens: those who are trying to protect one of the most amazing insect migrations on the planet.

This map from Monarch Watch shows the pattern of monarch migration in North America. Notice the smaller populations of monarchs living west of the Rockies and in Florida; these butterflies seem to follow different migration patterns from the larger northeastern population.

Monarch Butterfly
Fall & Spring Migrations

→	Fall migration
→	Spring migration
?	Unconfirmed
	Summer breeding areas
	Spring breeding areas
	Overwintering areas
	Corn belt: high monarch production

Northern range of milkweed

Contact zone between eastern and western populations

Pacific Ocean

SUMMER

WINTER

ROCKY MOUNTAINS

SUMMER

CORN BELT

SPRING

Atlantic Ocean

Gulf of Mexico

WINTER

WINTER

Monarch Watch.org
Education · Conservation · Research

If you live in the eastern United States, you can tag monarchs for Chip. If you live west or south of the Rocky Mountains, there are tagging programs for you, too. Learn more by visiting the Web sites listed in the back of this book. When you are ready, order some tags.

Get yourself a net. Find a good butterfly habitat. Come fall, start scanning the horizon for that telltale flurry of orange and black.

Do you see one?

Great.

Go get it!

MONARCH WATCHERS

A successful monarch tagging requires two citizen scientists: one to tag a butterfly at the beginning of its migration and one to collect its tag at the end. Meet two kids, one American and one Mexican, who have helped Chip and his team understand and protect the monarch butterfly migration.

Katie is seven years old and has been tagging monarch butterflies for more than half her life. (She started when she was three!) Rather than catching and tagging adult butterflies, Katie likes to collect late-season monarch caterpillars (that is, caterpillars that are part of the migrating generation of monarchs) and watch their life cycle unfold indoors. She provides them with a clean home and plenty of fresh milkweed leaves. When her caterpillars

Katie keeps her wild monarch caterpillars in clean cardboard containers, like this empty pretzel box.

Katie uses a pencil to help her manipulate the sticky tags.

Katie named the caterpillar that formed this pupa Princess Cutie Pie Pie, but the adult butterfly that emerged (can you see its orange and black wings through the pupal case?) had scent pouches. Princess Cutie Pie Pie was actually a prince!

become adult butterflies, Katie carefully records their sex, tags their wings, and releases them into the wild. None of Katie's tagged butterflies have yet been found in Mexico, but that doesn't stop her from watching and tagging each fall.

Daniel is six years old, and he lives with his family on one of the handful of mountains the monarchs flock to each winter. Throughout the winter months, Daniel, his sister, and their parents scour the forest floor for dead monarchs with tagged wings. When they find one, they remove the tag and store it with the others they've collected. Later in the spring, when Chip and his team of Monarch Watchers come to collect recovered tags, Daniel and his family turn theirs in. They are paid 50 pesos (about four American dollars) for each one.

For Daniel and his neighbors, collecting monarch butterfly tags is not a scientific adventure so much as a way to earn money for food and shelter. By paying for tags recovered in the wintering sites, Chip and his team have helped to build an economy around the butterflies, which serves as an incentive for local people and governments to protect butterflies and their habitat.

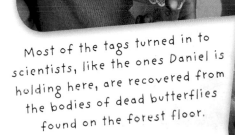

Most of the tags turned in to scientists, like the ones Daniel is holding here, are recovered from the bodies of dead butterflies found on the forest floor.

Occasionally citizen scientists return the entire butterfly body to Chip.

The sticky side of a recovered tag retains the telltale orange and black markings of a monarch butterfly (at left).

WHEN YOU GO...

Whether you plan to tag monarchs or not, an afternoon traipsing through field and meadow in search of butterflies is a grand adventure. There are about 700 species of butterflies to see in North America, and finding those that live in your neck of the woods can be both exhilarating and challenging. Here's a list of some things you'll want on your body or in your backpack the next time you head outside to butterfly:

A monarch caterpillar

- ☐ sturdy shoes
- ☐ long pants and long sleeves (to protect you from poison ivy and sharp prickers)
- ☐ bug spray (to protect you from mosquitoes and ticks—but don't put it on your hands if you plan to handle the butterflies you find)
- ☐ sunscreen and/or a hat
- ☐ water and a snack (but please remember to carry home any trash)
- ☐ binoculars and/or a camera
- ☐ a net (and tags, if you have them)
- ☐ a butterfly field guide
- ☐ a notebook and pen

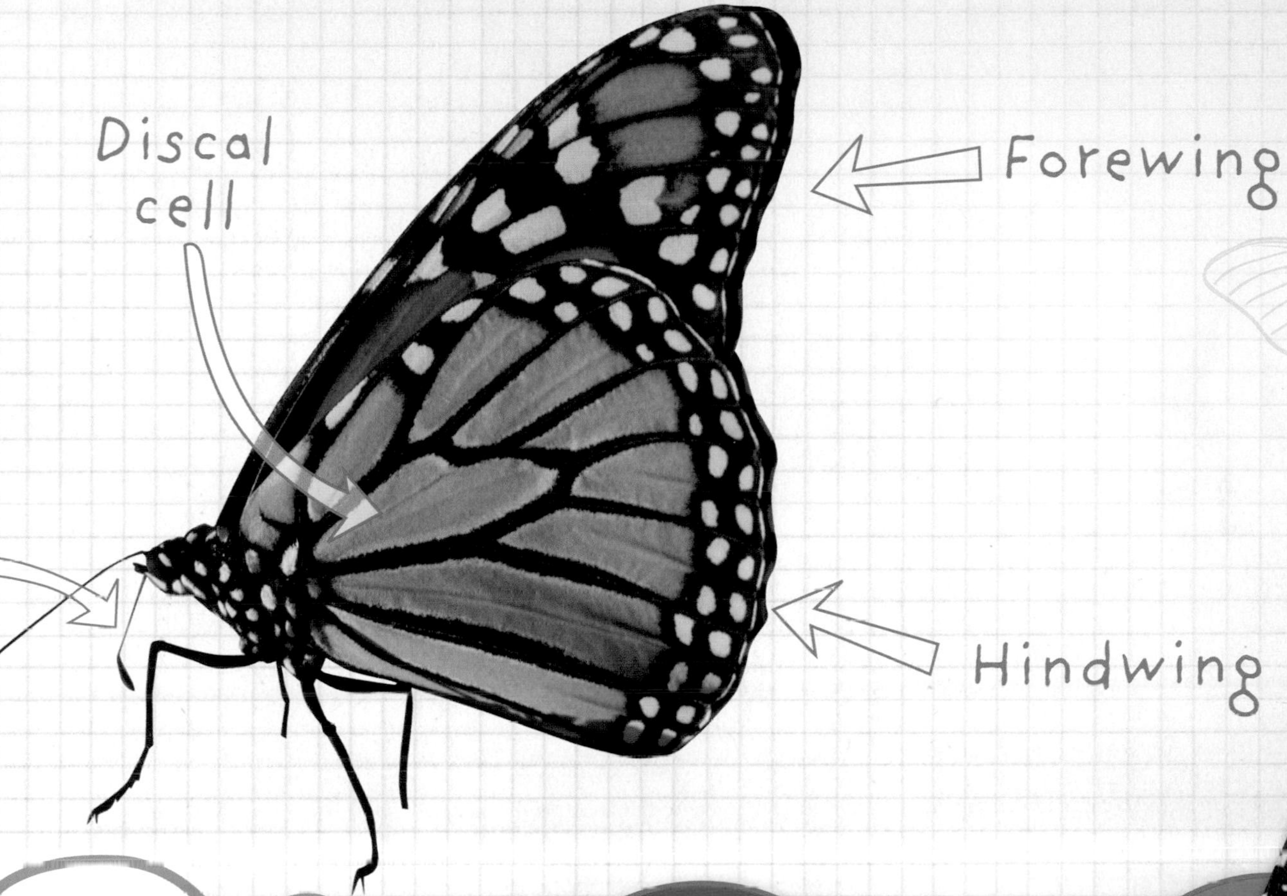

Discal cell

Forewing

Antennae

Hindwing

QUICK QUIZ

In the parts of the country where these four large, orange butterflies coexist, they can be tricky to tell apart in the field. Do you know which one is a monarch? Is it male or female? Can you name the other butterflies, too?

(Answers can be found on page 75.)

B

D

A

C

Bird feeders are a great way to attract birds to your backyard, school yard, or nearest green space. This one is filled with black-oil sunflower seeds (not visible) and a suet cake (center) and has attracted a black-capped chickadee (left) and an American goldfinch (right).

CHAPTER TWO
WINTER BIRDING

It's cold. You pull your hood up over your winter hat and curl your fingers into fists inside your mittens. You take a deep breath, wince at the bite in your chest, and wonder if your lungs could actually freeze. It's February in New England, and it is *cold*. Your neighbors are inside at this hour, probably still snuggling between flannel bedsheets. But not you. You're in the backyard, perched on top of last week's snowfall (six inches of powder, now frozen solid) with binoculars around your neck and the National Geographic Society's *Field Guide to the Birds of North America*

in your pocket. You can't believe you let your mom talk you into this. Speaking of whom . . .

"Okay, guys," she says. "I'm marking our start time as eight thirteen a.m. Let's count birds!"

You look at your brother, whose hat is almost covering his eyes, and shrug. He shrugs back, and you both turn to the house-shaped bird feeder at the back of the yard. Mom has kept the feeder full with seeds all winter, which is why there is so much activity this morning. The birds are feasting. As far as counting birds goes, the feeder is a sure thing.

"One chickadee," you tell Mom as you watch a small gray and white bird with a black cap fly in, grab a seed, and fly out again.

You recognize a few other birds up there, too.

"A goldfinch and another chickadee." These you list without even lifting your binoculars.

But suddenly there are three birds in the mix that you can't name. They're not much bigger than the chickadee, and are brown and stripy instead of gray. One of them has reddish feathers on its head and chest, and you guess that it's a male.

"What are those?" you ask no one in particular.

"Dunno," answers your brother. "House finches?"

Mom lifts her binoculars and points them in the direction of the feeder.

"Hmmmm. Either house finches or purple finches. The reddish one is a male." She scribbles on her clipboard. "I'll make a note, but we won't count them unless we figure out for sure what they are."

You pull out your field guide and sit down in the snow. House finches and purple finches are on the same page, and even after reading the descriptions and studying the drawings, you can't tell which you've got on your feeder. The guide says house finches have "squarish" tails and purple finches have "strongly notched" ones— but the tails in front of you won't stay still long enough for a good look. You're still trying when Mom calls the first count a wrap.

This citizen scientist is using a list of birds common to her geographical area and recording the highest number of individual birds of each species she sees at one particular time.

"That's it for this round," she says. "Who's up for some hot chocolate?"

Your family heads inside, but you stay behind to look at the mystery finches more closely. The male lands on the feeder tray again, and you wait, binoculars raised, for a glimpse of its tail feathers.

That's when the bigger bird arrives.

You only see it briefly: a blur on the right side of your binoculars and then a blur on the left side. You drop your glasses and scan the trees in that direction. Nothing. You study each tree from the ground slowly to the top. Still nothing. The hair on your neck is standing up, though, and it feels as if the entire yard —full of chips and chirps a minute ago—has gone quiet.

There!

On the leftmost tree, the skinny one, a bird's head peeks out. The first thing you notice: red. The second thing: big. At least compared with the chickadees and finches you've been looking at. As you raise your binoculars for a closer look, the bird climbs into full view.

There is a bright red stripe running from just

The red-bellied woodpecker is fairly common throughout the eastern United States.

above the bird's eyes, over the top of its head and down to the base of its neck. Sort of like a Mohawk. The rest of its face is white, as is its breast and belly. The back and wings are striped black and white, and the beak is large, black, and chiseled. You have never seen this bird before in your life.

"What the heck are you?" you ask out loud.

The bird is in constant motion. It moves up and around the tree trunk in tiny hops. Whenever its feet stop, its head starts moving: side to side, looking up, looking down, poking the bark of the tree. It's fascinating to watch, and you kind of forget that you're cold and there's hot chocolate in the house. Even when you hear footsteps crunching behind you, you keep your eyes on the bird.

"Shhhhh!" you whisper, and hold up your hand like a stop sign.

"What is it?" your brother whispers from several feet behind you.

"I don't know," you respond, handing him the field guide. "Maybe some kind of woodpecker."

While he flips through the guide, you describe what you've seen so far. And you continue to watch as the bird struts around the trunk, disappearing momentarily and reappearing on the opposite side. You wonder if there could be insects inside the bark of that tree, even in the cold.

"There! I think that's it!" your brother shouts as he smacks his gloved finger to a page.

"Shhhhh!"

Field guides are a great help with on-the-spot bird identification, but some birders prefer to sketch, photograph, or simply describe the birds they see in a journal; the task of correctly identifying them can be undertaken later, at home.

But it's too late. The bird is in flight, headed for the woods at the side of the yard. A second later, you lose sight of him.

"I think it was a red-bellied woodpecker," your brother whispers.

"You don't need to whisper now," you tell him. But you smile a little as you say it so that he knows you're not too mad. How *can* you be mad? You've just met a red-bellied woodpecker in your own backyard!

Do people actually do this—count birds in the middle of winter in the name of science? They sure do. In 2008, more than 60,000 people took part in the Audubon Society's Christmas Bird Count (CBC), and many of them counted in extreme winter weather. That's the thing about a scientific study: You can't change the rules on a whim. If you are part of a bird count team and it snows on the day you are supposed to count birds, well, you put on snow pants and go counting anyway.

Back in the late 1800s, bird *hunting* parties were much more common than bird *counting* parties. Groups of men and boys would gather for a day in the field shooting foxes, rabbits, bears, and game birds for both food and pelts. At Christmastime, these parties were especially exuberant, and it was not unusual for a group to split into teams and hunt in competition, a so-called match hunt. In the words of a prominent bird scientist of the day, Frank M. Chapman, the teams would "hie them to the fields and woods on the cheerful mission of killing practically everything in fur or feathers that crossed their path." Whichever side bagged the most animals was declared winner of the match hunt.

Winter is a good time to watch and count birds, especially in parts of the country where trees drop their leaves.

Not surprisingly, there were many people who thought this sort of sport was barbaric. Frank Chapman was one of them. In 1900, he came up with a plan to underscore the brutality of the Christmas match hunt and at the same time to encourage an interest in birds: a Christmas bird census. Instead of finding and shooting birds, Chapman invited outdoorsmen to find and *count* birds. He announced his idea in the pages of *Bird-Lore* magazine, hoping readers would be open to "spending a portion of Christmas Day with the birds and sending a report of their 'hunt' to *Bird-Lore* before retiring for the night." Twenty-five groups took up the challenge, and the results of their counts were soon published in the magazine.

Six years later, the number of Christmas Bird Count (CBC) reports had jumped to 135, and it has risen steadily since. These days, more than 2,000 CBC events are held annually, including counts in every state of the Union, every province of Canada, and even parts of Central and South America. The CBC is now the longest uninterrupted bird census in the world.

In suburban areas, bird counts are often conducted by car. Citizen scientists drive from street to street, stopping to count and record birds in neighborhoods (left) throughout their count circle. Sometimes (above) they even count birds from inside the car!

How does a Christmas Bird Count work? It's pretty easy. The Audubon Society has chosen specific areas across the continent, called count circles, in which to hold annual counts. Each circle is assigned a leader, or compiler, who organizes both the count and the information collected. (CBC events are no longer held on Christmas Day, by the way, but over a two-week period surrounding it.) On the day of a count, participants hike—or, in some cases, drive—assigned routes within their count circle,

Christmas Bird Count data has been used to track the expanding range of the tufted titmouse.
For the first 40 years of the count, titmice were never reported in the New England states;
today they are commonly spotted throughout New England.

tallying and recording the bird species they see along the way.

At the end of the day, numbers gathered within a circle are totaled; eventually they are added to a massive database of Christmas Bird Count results. In this way, each and every bird spotted during a CBC event becomes a piece of our planet's recorded history. How many tufted titmice were seen during the 1901 CBC in New York City's Central Park? Zero. How many tufted titmice were seen during the 2009 CBC in Central Park? One hundred eighty-three. These numbers are permanently recorded in the CBC database, and they will be available for scientists and citizens to study and ponder long after the men, women, and children who counted the individual titmice are gone.

The Christmas Bird Count is the oldest bird monitoring project in the United States, but it is no longer the only one. The Great Backyard Bird Count, Project FeederWatch, and a host of other national and regional projects welcome birders of all ages and

This sign celebrating citizen scientist Sarah Elliott marks the meeting spot for New York City's Central Park Christmas Bird Count event.

experience levels as citizen scientists. You can find information on these projects at the back of this book.

So, then, what are you up to this winter? Seen any birds hanging around your school yard or in the neighborhood park? Don't you think it's time you stopped and got to know a few of them?

BIRD COUNTERS

New York City's Central Park has hosted a Christmas Bird Count every single year since 1900. The counts were once the passion of one or two avid New York birders. These days, the event attracts a large, mixed crowd of both experienced and beginning birders. On the chosen day each December, birders gather at the south end of the park and split into seven groups. The groups fan out and scour every corner of Central Park for the rest of the morning, reassembling in the afternoon to tally their data.

At the 2008 event, several generations of New Yorkers worked side by side to record the park's winter bird population. It was 14-year-old Simon's second CBC event, and the frigid temperatures didn't bother him a bit.

"You block that out," he insists. "I never look as closely at anything as I do at birds through binoculars."

The Jacqueline Kennedy Onassis Reservoir in New York City's Central Park

Simon's mentor for the morning was David Krauss, a lifelong New Yorker with 28 Central Park Christmas Bird Counts to his credit. David volunteers each year to lead the group that counts around the Jacqueline Kennedy Onassis Reservoir, home to a large and diverse group of ducks and gulls.

"No one ever wants to do the reservoir," he says. "Most people don't want to see gulls and ducks; they want to see songbirds."

Those folks missed some amazing birds in 2008, though; Simon, David, and their reservoir team counted over 1,700 birds, including 8 bufflehead ducks, 23 hooded mergansers, and 525 ring-billed gulls.

Later in the day, inside the historic Arsenal Building, Simon and David joined other birders for a warm lunch, a compilation of the day's counts, and some words of inspiration from Irving Cantor, who has been part of Central Park's CBC team since 1935. Cantor told the gathered crowd that bird census work keeps him healthy.

"It's very valuable," he says. "It makes you aware of things, sharpens your senses. There are very few people my age, almost ninety years old, in the condition I'm in. The birding is part of it."

David Krauss uses a spotting scope to help him see ducks and gulls on the reservoir. Although you can't see it in this photograph, he also uses a handheld counting device.

Simon works with veteran bird counter Sarah Elliott to tally birds after the Central Park count.

WHEN YOU GO...

More than 800 species of birds live in or pass through North America each year. Only a small subset of these will be common where you live, though, so learning to identify a good number of them is actually possible. With practice, you'll learn to recognize birds by their size and shape, habitat, behaviors, and color patterns, known as field marks. Although winter is a popular season for bird census projects, you can watch—and count—birds any time of year. Here's a list of items to pack when you "hie to the fields and woods":

☐ winter gear, if needed, including hat, gloves, boots, and snow pants

☐ sunscreen and/or a hat

☐ binoculars and/or a camera

☐ a bird field guide

☐ a notebook and pencil (ink doesn't flow well in cold temperatures)

☐ a spotting scope and a handheld counting device (for experienced birders)

Crown

Nape

Bill

Back

Tail

Chin

Breast

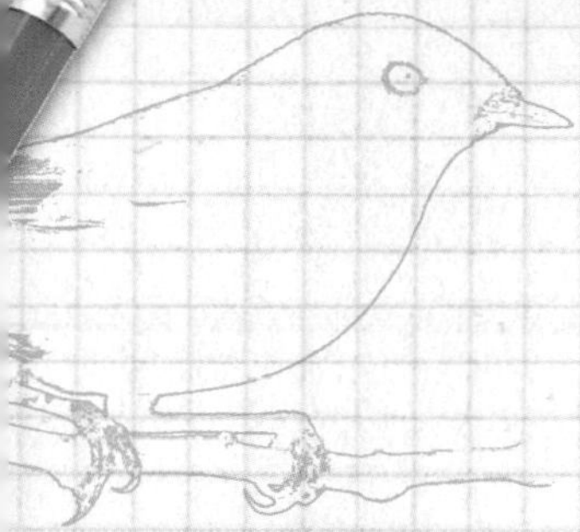

QUICK QUIZ

All four of these bird species have been recorded in New York City's Central Park in recent years. Have you seen them where you live? Can you name each species?

(Answers can be found on page 75.)

A

B

C

D

When was the last time you sat outside, looked at the
moon, and listened to the sounds of nighttime?

CHAPTER THREE
SPRING FROGGING

It all started with a lady at the end of the driveway on the first warm night of spring. She wasn't doing anything, just standing there outside her car with a clipboard in her hand and a flashlight on her head. You went out there with Dad to find out what she was up to, and the story she told was completely weird: She was counting frogs. Apparently, the easiest way to count frogs is to listen for the mating calls they make after the sun goes down.

Who knew?

And here's the thing: Now that you know, you can't stop thinking about it. You found a book at the library that shows photos of all the frogs and toads in your area, and it came with a CD. The calls are amazing, and you've gotten good at imitating a few of them. In fact, you're pretty sure that if you did your American toad impersonation while the frog lady was in the driveway, she would count *you*.

Memorizing which call belongs to which frog is much harder. After a week with the library CD, though, you've got them all down. It was a matter of associating each call with a certain sound.

- American toad—a high-pitched raspberry that goes on and on and on;

- gray tree frog—a shorter and wobblier raspberry;

- Fowler's toad—your baby sister screaming;

- green frog—a one-stringed banjo;

- northern leopard frog—an old door *creeeaaaking* open;

- American bullfrog—a cow with a super-deep voice and a knack for hypnotic, rhythmic mooing;

- eastern spadefoot toad—like an American bullfrog with a head cold;

- pickerel frog—a thumb running down the edge of a pocket comb;

- wood frog—a duck quacking;

- spring peeper (a kind of frog)—a newborn chick chirping sweetly, at least until you get a crowd of them together, in which case they sound more like a scene from *Attack of the Killer Birds*.

You tested your listening skills with an online frog call quiz and aced it. You're actually pretty good at this! Spring has barely gotten started where you live, and you don't know if or when the frog lady will be back, so you take the leap and become a frog watcher yourself.

You practically bounce outside the first night the thermometer inches over 35° Fahrenheit. (You've learned that frogs don't call when it's colder than that.) It's dark on the porch, and quiet. You listen intently for three minutes.

Then three more.

And three more after that.

Thirty minutes later, you're getting stiff and there hasn't been a single interesting sound. You flick on your flashlight and check the thermometer again: 32°. Ack! Too cold. Frog watching is not as easy as you thought it would be.

It stays cold for several days. Finally, nearly one week after your first trip onto the porch, you step out there again. It's 40° and the air is damp. The sun hasn't quite set yet, and you know by now that the temperature will drop several

As if learning to identify frogs and toads by their mating calls weren't hard enough, amphibian watchers must learn to take notes in the dark.

drone of traffic on a far-off highway, the neighbor's front door opening and then slamming shut. Silence. But somewhere in that unusual quiet you suddenly hear a short *pip* of a noise. Again. Now two, in quick succession. Spring peepers! You look at your watch and start the timer.

Over the next three minutes, you hear several peepers. They never build up to much, certainly not the choruses you've heard on the CD, but you're pretty sure there are more than two out there. Peepers. Calling for mates. Somewhere nearby.

Listening carefully takes practice. If you have trouble, try closing your eyes; some people find this makes it easier to focus their attention on sounds.

degrees when it does. Still, you're hopeful that tonight is the night you'll hear some frog calls.

Sitting in the dusk, you close your eyes and practice focusing on your other senses. The faintest breeze brushes the right side of your face. The air smells woodsy and wet, almost moldy. Dishes clink as someone inside loads the dishwasher, and you can just make out the muffled sound of a radio. You let those noises drift into the background, force your ears to search for other sounds. There aren't many: the

Every day, the peepers get a little louder. The next time you step onto the porch to record them, they are calling before the sun has even set. By the time it's fully dark, their racket has taken over the yard. If there are other frogs calling, you can't hear them. Heck, your baby sister could be babbling beside you, and you wouldn't hear her either. Peepers are LOUD.

The next week: peepers again. You do a second and then a third three-minute calling window, trying hard to hear other sounds in the midst of the chirping peepers. You close your eyes and cup your hands around your ears. Finally you do pick up another sound, a muffled sort of quack. You focus completely on this new sound, straining to reach it. It takes time, but eventually you're sure. Wood frogs. Quacking in the dark.

By the end of June you've gotten good at listening, and you've recorded all sorts of sounds: windows sliding up and down, a motorcycle, a neighbor's table saw, a dog barking, cats fighting, geese honking, crickets fiddling, mosquitoes buzzing, an owl hooting. You've heard the rustling of some kind of animal in the brush, seen its gleaming eyes staring at you from the woods (a raccoon? a fox?). And you've learned that at least four species of frogs live and mate within hearing distance of your back porch.

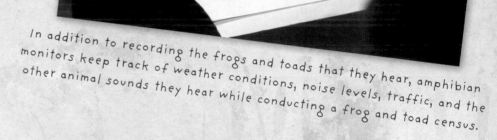

In addition to recording the frogs and toads that they hear, amphibian monitors keep track of weather conditions, noise levels, traffic, and the other animal sounds they hear while conducting a frog and toad census.

You've learned other things, too: how long three minutes can feel when you're sitting in the dark, how an entire world awakens outside when the sun goes down, how human sounds can scare a thriving frog chorus into silence, and how to wait out this silence. You've learned how to take notes when you can't see the notepaper in front of you, or even the pen in your hand. You've learned how to sit and search at the same time.

In one wild spring, you have learned to see in the dark—and that you don't need eyes to do it.

Frog watching as a citizen science project has its roots, at least partially, in a school field trip. In 1995, a group of sixth-, seventh-, and eighth-graders in Minnesota went on a hike with their teacher, Mrs. Reinitz. She had planned a hike, but on the way to the trail, the students came across an army of frogs. Who can resist the temptation of a hopping frog? Within minutes, three different students had captured a frog. The world was never quite the same again.

Why? Because all three of those captured frogs were badly deformed.

Mrs. Reinitz and her class forgot all about their hike and instead spent the morning running around after frogs. They caught 22 in all, 11 of which had missing or abnormal hind legs. Intrigued and worried, they brought several of the frogs back to school in order to photograph them. Then they shared the pictures and their story with local scientists.

Over the course of the next four years, outbreaks of deformed frogs were reported elsewhere in Minnesota and, in fact, around the country. A number of top researchers and government organizations worked furiously to understand the outbreaks. A parasitic worm was eventually blamed for at least some of the frog deformities. A fungus that infects and kills frogs has also been discovered, though, and additional studies suggest that chemical contaminants in the environment are harming frog and toad populations, too. Although scientists don't always agree on which of these problems is hardest on amphibian

populations, one thing is clear: We humans ought to keep a closer watch on the frogs and toads in our world. The North American Amphibian Monitoring Program (NAAMP) and FrogWatch USA, launched in 1997 and 1998, respectively, are citizen science projects designed to do just that.

In both cases, amphibian monitoring is accomplished without actually seeing the animals. Instead, participants listen for the calls male frogs and toads make to attract females during the mating season. Frog watchers must learn the calls of all the frogs and toads in their area. And because the various species mate at different times during the season, participants must also monitor their locations regularly from early spring until late summer. This ensures that the full cast of local frog and toad species are recorded. (By the way, toads are simply a family of warty, short-legged frogs, so the phrase "frog watch" refers to people monitoring both frogs and toads.)

Learning frog calls takes dedication, as does following through on a weekly frog call survey. But thousands of kids and adults do it every year, and the result is a growing database of information on local frog populations throughout the country. Although this database is quite small compared with 50 years of monarch tagging data and 100 years of bird counting data, with enough time and enough volunteers, the NAAMP and FrogWatch programs will begin helping scientists understand how frog populations change over time.

This American toad—like most toads—has warty skin and lives its adult life on dry land, often far from the wetlands in which it was born. Adult frogs, on the other hand, have smoother skin and tend to live near water.

This pond is home to several species of frogs; adults are often found in the shallow, weedy area along the pond's edge.

45

Of course, many frog watchers—professional amphibian scientists and amateur citizen scientists alike—prefer to study frogs by day. And this is fine; monitoring frogs and toads visually is equally important work. Just remember that now is a difficult time in the natural history of the frog. If you catch one in the wild, be gentle. Learn what you can and then release your frog *exactly* where you found it. Do what you can to keep its home—your local wetland ecosystem—clean

This beauty is a green frog, known to scientists by the name *Rana clamitans*. Despite the name, green frogs are not always green!

African clawed frogs are used in research labs around the world and are common pet store frogs. Intentional or accidental release into the wild has led to stable populations in the southwestern United States, where these voracious predators compete with native frogs for food and other resources.

and protected. And never, ever release a pet store frog into the wild, as this can lead to populations that threaten native frogs by competing with them for food and shelter. You might also consider reporting the frogs and toads you see during the day to the National Wildlife Federation Wildlife Watch program.

So, are you the sort of person who—like Mrs. Reinitz's middle school students—would be distracted by a parade of hopping frogs and excited by the idea of helping them? Do you like being out of doors, even at night? Are you intrigued by the thought of listening to spring? Have you held a frog or toad in your hand, looked it in the eye, and felt something?

Excellent!

You are a natural frog watcher. Wild springs await you.

Vernal pools are bodies of water that exist only for part of the year, usually forming in the spring and drying up by the end of summer. The author visits them often to look—and listen!—for frogs.

FROG LOVERS

Mariah started watching frogs at the age of four, when she found some bullfrog tadpoles in a pond. Now a high school student, she has made her frog-watching status official: She and her mother, Joyce, have been FrogWatch citizen scientists since the spring of 2008.

"It's not a very hard thing to do," Mariah says. "If I am coming home from dance class and we drive by a pond, we always slow down to see if the frogs are peeping. If we hear them, we stop and turn the car off and listen. It only takes five minutes. It's easy for a family that does a lot of other stuff."

She admits that memorizing the calls can be difficult, but she and her mother have stumbled upon the perfect solution for that: They travel

While it's okay to take a closer look a frogs and toads in the wild, be sure t release them immediately—and exactl where you found them.

Mariah and Peeper, her pet Australian white tree frog.

with a recorder. Whenever they hear a frog call they are unable to identify, they record it, take it home, and compare it with frog and toad recordings online. Mother and daughter have also learned to vary their frog watching—or listening—to keep things interesting.

"If we go before sunset, we might hear a couple of brave frogs, but you're not going to hear what you'd hear later at night," Mariah says. These daylight expeditions, however, are great for catching and identifying frog species by sight. On days when Mariah and Joyce don't get outside until after dark, they listen for frog calls and record species by sound instead.

"FrogWatch is something that I can do to help the frogs," says Mariah.

A tadpole

A mass of frog eggs

Amphibian monitoring, like all citizen science projects, is a great family activity. In this image, Mariah and Joyce are reflected in their favorite frog pond.

WHEN YOU GO...

Since frog monitoring happens mostly at night, special safety precautions are in order. If you're going to monitor frogs outside your backyard, you should always work with a partner. If you will be working near roads, be sure your clothing makes you visible to drivers. Carry a flashlight. (Better yet, carry two flashlights—and a spare set of batteries, too!) Expect curious looks from strangers and be prepared to explain what you are up to. In addition to these commonsense safety practices, you may want to have these items on hand:

☐ a raincoat or an umbrella
☐ long pants and long sleeves (to protect you from poison ivy)
☐ bug spray (but don't put it on your hands if you plan to handle frogs)
☐ extra batteries for your flashlight
☐ a watch for timing how long you listen for frog calls
☐ a cell phone and/or a recording device
☐ a frog and toad field guide
☐ a notebook and pen (as always!)

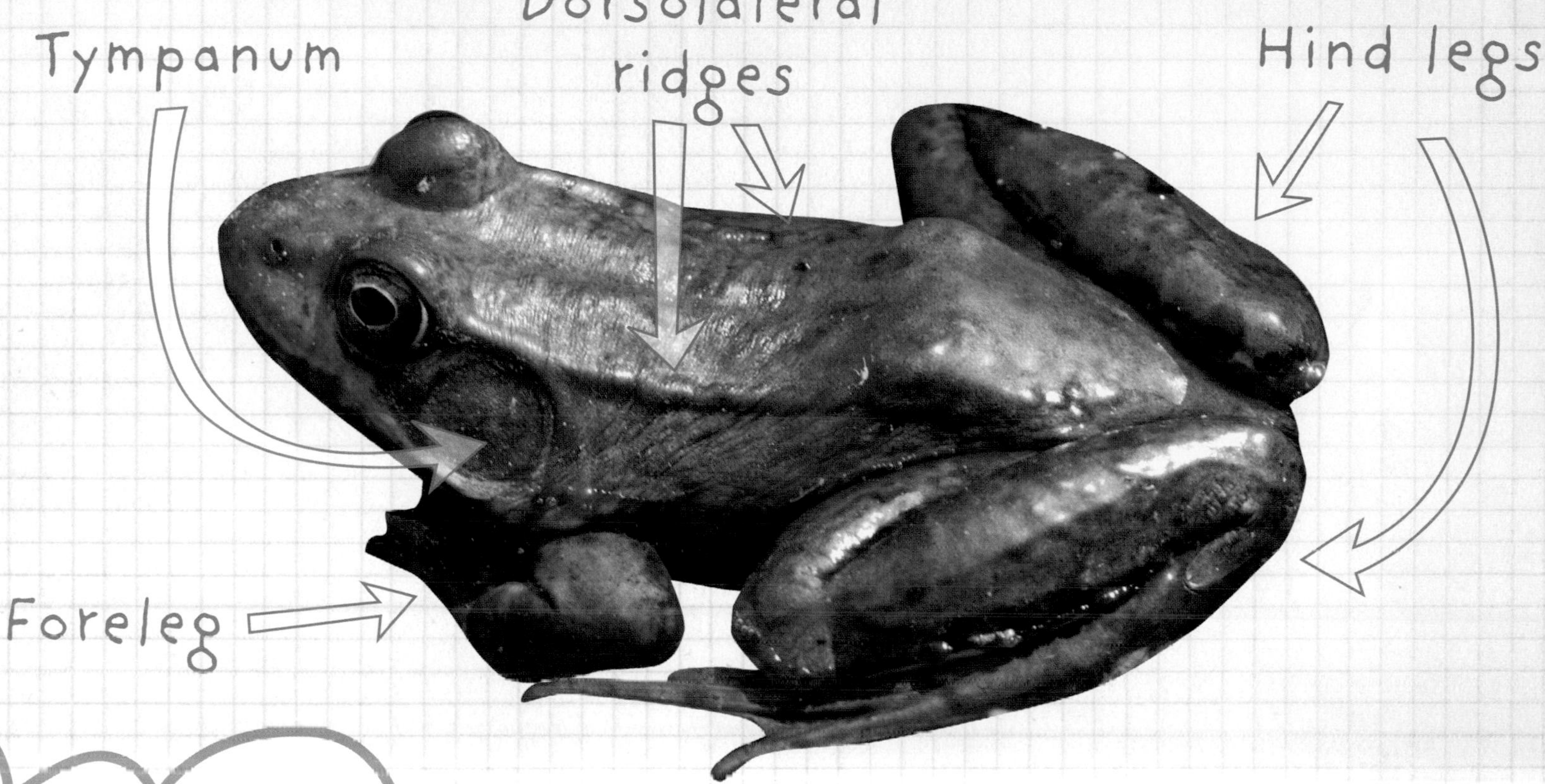

Tympanum

Dorsolateral ridges

Hind legs

Foreleg

QUICK QUIZ

Like the other animals described in this book, individual frog and toad species have specific ranges. There are over 100 species in North America, but only a handful of those will make a home in your geographical area. These frogs live in specific parts of the United States. Do you recognize any of them?

(Answers can be found on page 75.)

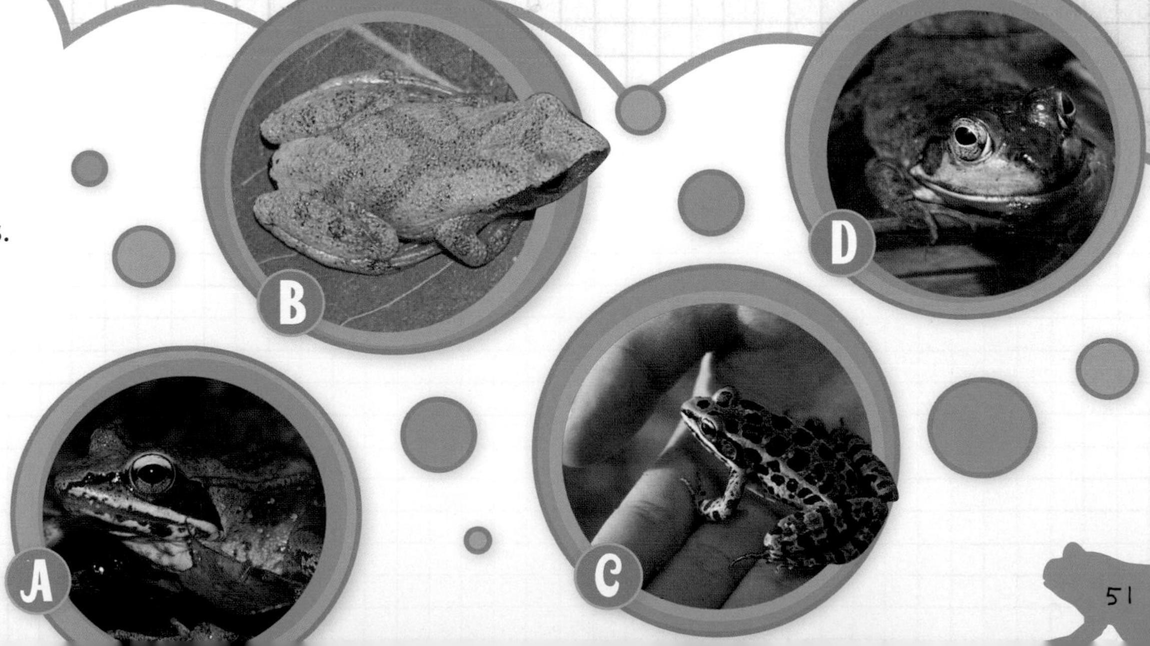

B

D

A

C

Sweep nets look like butterfly nets but are made with a rougher fabric meant for wrestling with tall grasses and woody shrubs.

52

CHAPTER FOUR

SUMMER LADYBUGGING

As the school bus pulls to the side of the road, you can't help but stare out the window. Your teacher wasn't kidding. He told you and your classmates before the bus left school that this field trip was to an actual field and that you'd be learning how to shoot lady-bugs. You thought he was joking. But now the bus is parked beside a rectangle of clover plants set amid a huge expanse of other green fields, and you wonder: Could he have been serious about shooting ladybugs, too?

He was. But once you're all off the bus and assembled beside the field, he explains that the shooting will be done with a digital camera . . . of course. You'll each have a chance to gather insects from the field, sort through them for ladybugs, and photograph the ones you find.

"The ladybugs will stay here," he explains, "but we'll take the photographs back to school so that we can properly identify them. Then we'll send our images to scientists who are keeping track of North American ladybug species."

53

Just when you thought the day couldn't possibly be more interesting, he hands you a net with a long, wooden handle.

"It's a sweep net," he says. "Follow me."

And then he plunges into the clover! You watch in amazement as he sweeps his net firmly from side to side while marching toward the opposite end of the field.

You glance at a bee buzzing around the purple blossom by your left knee.

You glance at your classmates, who are mostly wide-eyed.

Then you turn to the field, take a deep breath, and step into the world of ladybug research.

As you high-step through the clover, you concentrate on keeping your net moving. It's not as easy as it looks. Your teacher calls out encouragement from the middle of the field, where he's stopped to watch.

"Nice work!" he says when you reach him. "This time, try to alternate your sweeps, sometimes sweeping high up on the plants, sometimes sweeping down low." You have just enough time to turn yourself around and shuffle a few paces to the left before he begins blazing a new trail, this time back in the direction of your classmates.

At the edge of the field, he steps out and holds his net upright and away from his body. This, he explains, gives stinging insects time to fly out of the net. You do the same. In a short minute, he declares it safe and sticks his entire face into his net. You wait for him to emerge safely before taking a cautious peek inside your own. Yep. Bugs. Lots of them.

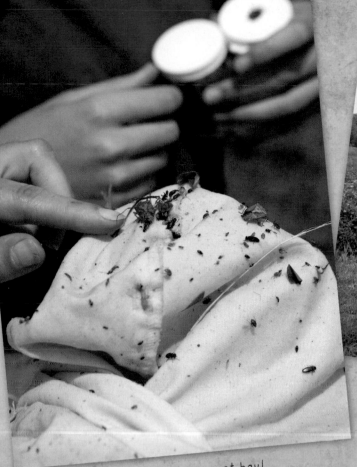

A sample sweep net haul

A convenient way to examine the contents of your sweep net is to empty it into a light-colored plastic bin.

"Now we sort them," your teacher says. He grabs a white plastic bin from the stack by his feet and shakes the contents of his net into it. Then he kneels down and begins sorting bugs with his bare hands; the entire class—including you—moves in for a closer look. Somehow he knows every creature on sight: a stinkbug nymph, a leafhopper, a lacewing, a fly, a fly larva, another lacewing, several grasshoppers, a crab spider, a soldier beetle, three tiny aphids. These last ones truly excite him.

"You know what this means, right?" he asks.

You don't. Judging by the quiet, neither does anyone else in the class.

"Ladybugs!" he says.

This ladybug goes by several names: checkerspot ladybug, taxicab ladybug, 14-spotted ladybug, and *Propylea quatuordecimpunctata.* Although the common names are easier to say, in different parts of the world the same common name could actually refer to a different ladybug; the scientific name is always the most reliable.

"Is it dead?" you ask.

"No. But it's pretending to be. Ladybugs will do that."

As if on cue, tiny legs peek out and it begins to move across his hand. He grabs a vial, unscrews the lid with his free hand, and pops the checkerspot inside. He passes the vial around and says the ladybug's scientific name out loud:

"*Propylea quatuordecimpunctata.*"

You try to repeat it but can't quite. Checkerspot it is.

By the time his bin is empty, there are four vials making their way around the circle: two checkerspot ladybugs, one multicolored Asian ladybug (*Harmonia axyridis*), and one pink-spotted ladybug (*Coleomegilla maculata*). Your teacher is being bombarded with questions. . . .

"How many different ladybugs are there?"

In this part of North America, about 70 species.

"How do you tell them apart?"

By their markings, mostly, although it can be tricky because some species come in many different color patterns.

Then he explains that ladybugs eat aphids, which is why farmers and gardeners like them so much. Wherever you find aphids, he insists, you'll find ladybugs. Sure enough, the very next creature out of the bin is a ladybug.

"This is a checkerspot," he says, placing it carefully in the palm of his hand. It lies still.

"Doesn't the number of spots tell you how old they are?"

No. That's an old wives' tale.

"Are all ladybugs ladies?"

No. That's an old wives' tale, too.

As he answers questions, he hands out ladybug field guides, empty vials, and magnifying glasses. Eventually he holds the two nets in the air and asks, "Who wants to sweep next?"

There is a roar of excitement. Those who don't get a net are divided into bug sorters and picture takers. You're still holding a net full of crawling insects, so you grab a bin and get busy. It doesn't take long to find your first ladybug, though it isn't quite like the four you've already seen today. The idea that you've found a new species flits into your head. You try to get a closer look with a magnifying glass, but you discover that when they aren't pretending to be dead, ladybugs are surprisingly fast. Even on the glass walls of a vial, your ladybug moves too quickly for you to study it.

You're wondering how you'll ever manage to get a picture of your little speed crawler when

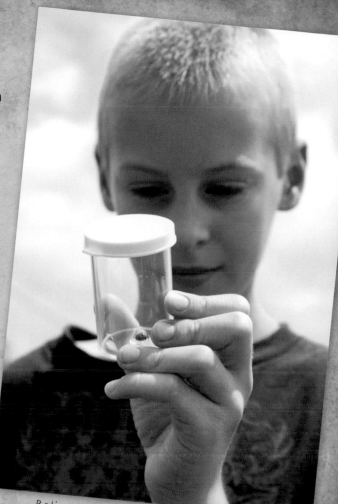

Believe it or not, there is enough air in this vial for the ladybug inside to survive for several days.

your teacher walks by with the part of the class assigned to photography. He sets a cooler on the ground and starts setting up his camera on a tripod.

"Put it in there," he says, pointing at the cooler. "We'll chill it with the others."

Chill it?

It turns out that briefly chilling ladybugs is harmless . . . and it slows them down. The easiest technique is to place a vial in the freezer for exactly five minutes, but that isn't possible out here in the field. Instead, you bury your vial deep in the ice-filled cooler and wait a bit longer. In 30 minutes, your ladybug's tiny body is cooled to the point of stillness. You tap it out onto a sheet of paper, breathe a sigh of relief when it lands spotted side up, and start shooting. Before you click the shutter for a third time, though, the little bugger has regained its senses. You wrestle it back into the vial and hope your pictures are good enough.

The rest of the morning is a frenzy of sweeping, sorting, and shooting. Somehow you and your classmates collect a total of seven different ladybug species. (And to think that when you arrived here this morning you thought there was only one!) When it's time to go, your teacher hands back the vials and you release the captured ladybugs into the field.

On the bus ride back to school, you and your classmates agree: This was the best field trip ever. Kids wonder out loud about the number of ladybug species you might have found if you'd had more time, and a couple of your classmates beg for a return trip to the clover. Your teacher tells the entire bus about some very rare ladybug species and how kids like you are helping scientists learn about them. While he is talking, you remember something he said earlier: Wherever you find aphids you'll find ladybugs.

Dr. John Losey and his Lost Ladybug Project team have engineered a field camera that allows them to photograph ladybugs without chilling them. The white tube under the camera lens has a screen for the ladybug to rest on and is hooked to a small vacuum pump which, when turned on, holds the ladybug in place.

You've seen plenty of aphids at your house, and you've heard your mother complain about them being on her rosebushes. That's when it hits you: You don't need a field trip to study ladybugs, or even a field. You could study them in your own backyard.

Dr. John Losey had been studying ladybugs in New York State for years when he began to wonder about one species in particular, the nine-spotted ladybug. Called C-9 for short (or *Coccinella novemnotata* for long), the nine-spotted ladybug is the official state insect of New York, but John hadn't seen one in the field for a long while. In fact, a thorough review of published ladybug surveys turned up this interesting fact: No one else had either. In 2007, when John published these findings, New York's state insect hadn't been collected inside state lines for more than 30 years!

John identified two other ladybug species that had once been common in the northeastern United States and were now quite hard to find: the transverse ladybug (*Coccinella transversoguttata*) and the two-spotted ladybug (*Adalia bipunctata*). He and others began to wonder if these three species of ladybug were extinct.

"I wanted to find out if they were really gone," Dr. Losey says, "or if they were just less common than they used to be."

Searching the range for these three rare ladybugs was going to be difficult—he was, after all, only one man, and the ladybugs had once been found across most of the United States. John knew he'd need some extra eyes and hands in the field looking with him. So he turned to people who spend a lot of time outside and who are typically pretty excited about nature. He turned to kids.

His idea was simple: Create a Web site where kids (and their adults) could learn the basics of ladybug biology, and then encourage them to get outside and photograph the ladybugs in their backyards, school playgrounds, and local parks. John asked users to upload their digital images to his Web site, and in return, he and his team of experts would help identify the ladybugs they found. Together, scientists and citizens would create a detailed map of ladybug diversity across the continent.

Citizen scientists found all three of the original "lost ladybugs," including a two-spotted ladybug (*Adalia bipunctata*; above), in Naches, Washington; a transverse ladybug (*Coccinella transversoguttata*; top right), in Falcon, Colorado; and a nine-spotted ladybug (*Coccinella novemnotata*; bottom right), also in Falcon, Colorado.

Since its launch, the Lost Ladybug Project has received thousands of images from citizen scientists across the country. Ladybugs from every state in the Union are listed in its database, and among them are 96 different species . . . including all three of the lost ladybugs. The nine-spotted ladybug, the transverse ladybug, and the two-spotted ladybug are officially found again, although they are much rarer than they used to be.

Does this mean John's work with the project is over? Not a chance. Citizen scientists have proven that these three ladybug species are not extinct, but there is still much to learn about what is happening to them in the wild.

"Are there places these ladybugs still have viable populations and are doing okay?" John wonders. "Or can we halt their decline? Can we reverse it? How can we keep this decline from happening to other ladybug species?"

The answers to these questions will almost certainly be revealed through the continued work of John's nationwide team of ladybug spotters. Using the information they submit, John and his colleagues have created new range maps that show where the nine-spotted, transverse, and two-spotted ladybugs are most likely to be found. As more and more specimens are photographed and submitted, the scientists fine-tune their maps.

This map of North America shows where rare ladybugs have been found by Lost Ladybug Project participants as of October 2009.

The Lost Ladybug Project team uses these props when visiting classrooms and nature centers to recruit citizen scientists to their project.

Analyzing the project data also helps John and his colleagues better understand other factors that may affect the rare species, including competition from other ladybugs. More than half of the ladybug images submitted to the project in its first two years were of invasive species—ladybugs that are not native to North America. These foreign ladybugs were brought to this country several decades ago in the hope that they would halt the spread of crop pests. The ladybugs did stop the pests, but they became so well established in their new homeland that they are now the most commonly sighted ladybugs in the wild. In fact, 37 percent of the ladybugs photographed for the Lost Ladybug Project in 2008 and 2009 were multicolored Asian ladybugs (*Harmonia axyridis*), one of these introduced species.

John and his students at Cornell have figured out how to raise multicolored Asian ladybugs in a laboratory setting and, using tips from ladybug spotters, are trying to establish colonies of rare native species as

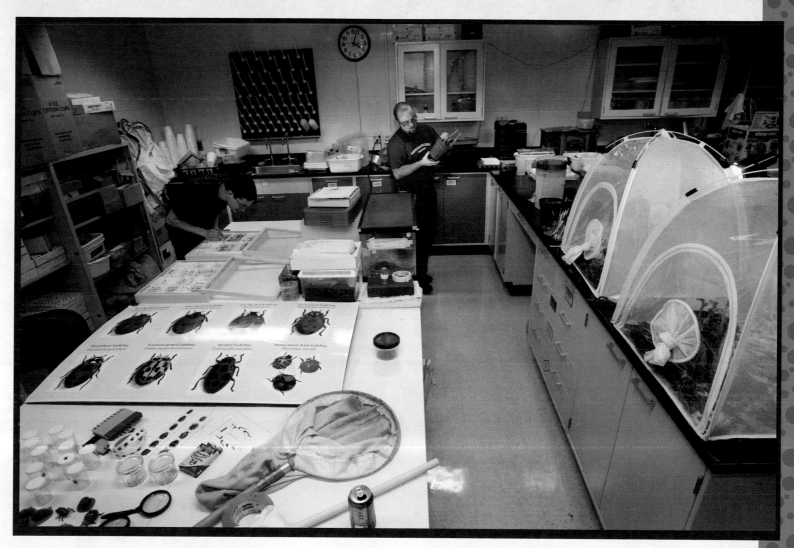

John Losey's laboratory at Cornell University: The tents (right) hold colonies of the multicolored Asian ladybug (*Harmonia axyridis*), and the glass tanks on the table (center) hold eggs and larvae of rare ladybugs.

well. They plan to study how these species interact in captivity and, eventually, how they compete in the wild. All this work is dependent upon the contributions of ladybug citizen scientists.

"With information that kids have supplied," John says, "we are starting to get a really good handle on where our rare ladybugs are."

And by now, of course, you realize (don't you?) that one of the most intriguing places they might be is in your own backyard.

LADYBUG FINDERS

It was John Losey's own son, Ben, who helped him realize that kids could become top spotters in the Lost Ladybug Project. Ben found his first rare ladybug—or rather, it found him—when he was four years old.

"We were in South Dakota, and I was just sitting on the grass, and a ladybug happened to crawl up on me. It was a two-spot," Ben remembers.

His next big find was a transverse ladybug, also quite rare, collected in Wyoming while on a trip with his dad.

Other kids have made important ladybug finds, too. Back in 2006, Jilene (then 11 years old) and her brother Jonathan (then 10) found the first nine-spotted ladybug documented in eastern North America in more than 14 years. And they found it simply by exploring their Virginia backyard.

SCIENTIST REGISTRATION

In addition to hunting ladbugs, Jilene and Jonathan have counted bees and other creatures for a biodiversity program near their home.

Ladybug pupa

In 2009, Alyson (then six years old) found all three of the rare native ladybug species—a nine-spotted, a two-spotted, and a transverse ladybug—in the woods behind her Oregon home. John and his team were so excited that they flew to Oregon to look for ladybugs in her backyard, too.

The bottom line is that anyone of any age can spot ladybugs. Finding rare species is always exciting, but not finding them is equally important to John Losey and his colleagues.

"One of the things we need to make our range maps better," says John, "is for people to report when they go out and don't find rare ladybugs. Those are actually important collections of data."

Whenever citizen scientists hunt ladybugs and then report to John how intensely they hunted and what they found—even if what they found was nothing—they advance our knowledge of ladybugs. Each ladybug hunt, successful or not, improves the overall picture of which ladybugs are out there and what is happening with them.

Ladybug larva

John Losey and Alyson hunt ladybugs in Oregon.

Despite his expertise in ladybugs, Ben's favorite insect is the rhinoceros beetle.

WHEN YOU GO...

Although classroom groups often visit an agricultural field or a meadow and use sweep nets to survey ladybugs, some people prefer simply to scour these places visually and take pictures of ladybugs in their natural positions in the environment. One advantage to this technique is that chasing and/or chilling the ladybugs isn't necessary, and an undisturbed ladybug on a plant moves much more slowly than one that has been collected by hand and placed in front of a camera. Either way, you'll want to take along these supplies the next time you pack up for a ladybugging expedition:

☐ bug spray (again, don't put bug spray on your hands if you plan to handle the insects you find)

☐ sunscreen and/or a hat

☐ a camera

☐ a magnifying glass

☐ a sweep net

☐ collection vials (small plastic food storage containers will do)

☐ ice in a cooler (if you plan to chill and photograph ladybugs)

☐ a ladybug field guide

☐ a notebook and pen

* Advanced ladybugsters might also include a beating tray and/or beating stick. These are used to collect insects from trees and sturdy shrubs. The tray— a simple square of light-colored cloth stretched over a wooden frame—is held under a tree limb while the stick is used to shake it. Insects on the limb drop onto the tray, where they can be observed and identified.

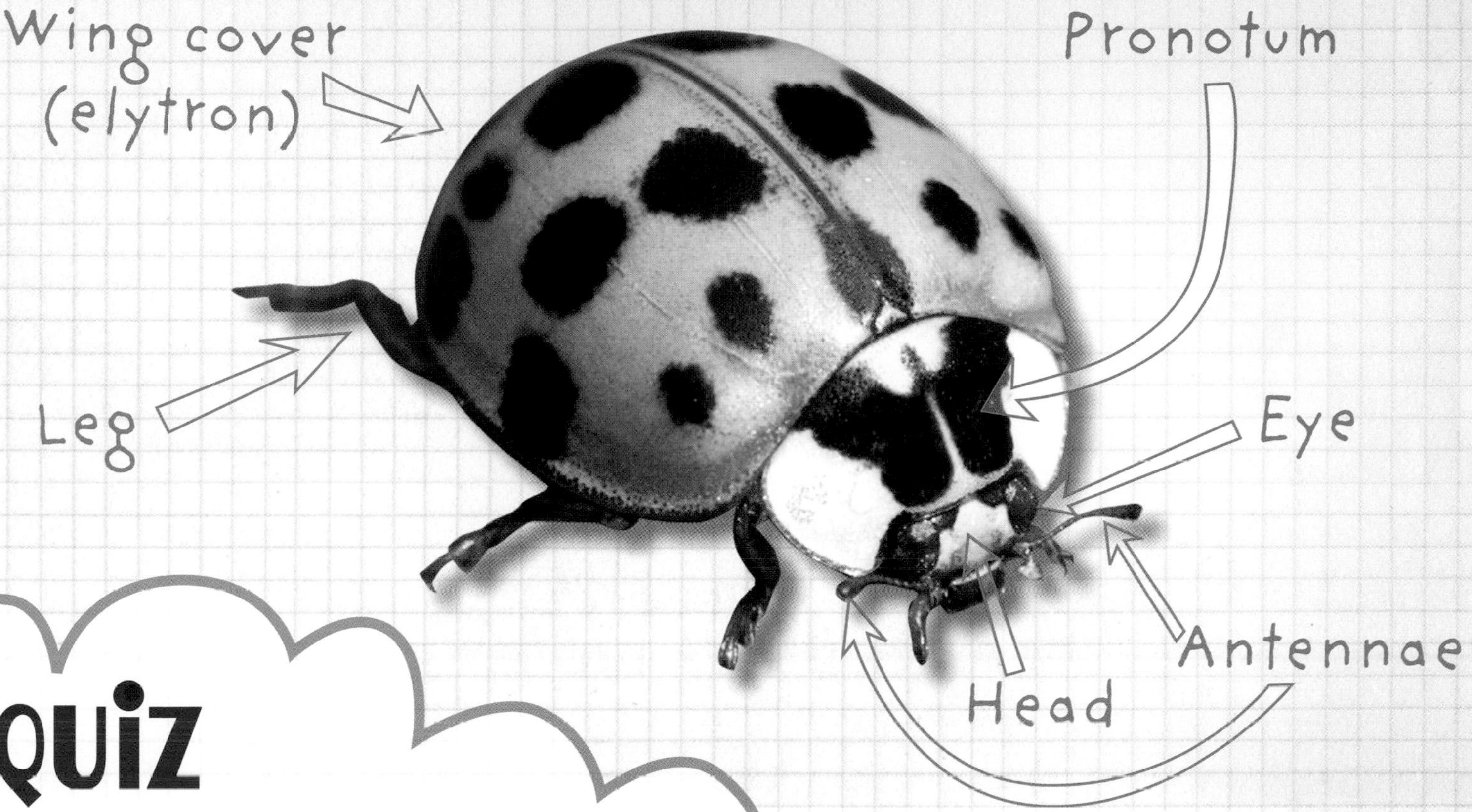

Wing cover
(elytron) ⇨

Pronotum

Leg ⇨

Eye

Antennae

Head

QUICK QUIZ

Have ladybugs ever covered the outside of your house on a warm fall day? Or found their way inside? In both cases, the ladybug in question is most likely the multicolored Asian ladybug. In Asia, this species seeks out a winter resting place in the cracks and crevices of vertical cliff faces. Scientists suspect that when they flock to the outside of your house (a vertical cliff face, of sorts) they are looking for a place to spend the winter. If they find cracks and crevices, they head on in. These images include two multicolored Asian ladybug specimens; can you identify them? Can you identify the other species as well? (Answers can be found on page 75.)

A

B

C

D

Got dandelions in your yard? You can study
them for the scientists who run Project Budburst.
This and many other citizen science projects are listed
in the resources pages at the back of this book.

NOW WHAT?

This is the sort of book that is likely to generate just as many questions as it answers. I hope that excites you! To get you started on finding the answers you need, I've provided a list of resources—books and field guides and Internet sites—that can help you learn more about butterflies, birds, frogs, ladybugs, and citizen science. These resources are great places to begin, but studying them won't be nearly as fun as loading your backpack and stepping out into the wild, senses at the ready. There is so much out there waiting to be wondered about and understood, and you, my friend, are just the kid to wonder and understand.

Happy exploring!

BUTTERFLY ReSOURCeS

BOOKS

An Extraordinary Life: The Story of a Monarch Butterfly, by Laurence Pringle and Bob Marstall (Orchard, 1997)

Monarchs, by Kathryn Lasky and Christopher G. Knight (Harcourt, 1993)

*Do Butterflies Bite? Fascinating Answers to Questions about Butterflies and Moths, by Hazel Davies and Carol A. Butler (Rutgers University Press, 2008)

FIELD GUIDES

The Life Cycles of Butterflies: From Egg to Maturity, a Visual Guide to 23 Common Garden Butterflies, by Judy Burris and Wayne Richards (Storey, 2006)

*Milkweed, Monarchs, and More: A Field Guide to the Invertebrate Community in the Milkweed Patch, by Ba Rea, Karen Oberhauser, and Michael A. Quinn (Bas Relief Publishing, 2003)

*National Audubon Society Field Guide to North American Butterflies, edited by Robert Michael Pyle (Knopf, 1981)

INTERNET ReSOURCeS

There are several organizations that sponsor monarch tagging programs in the United States; deciding which program is best for you depends on what part of the country you live and butterfly in.

Monarch Watch:

www.monarchwatch.org

This is the most comprehensive monarch tagging program. Because its goal is to understand and preserve the migration of eastern monarchs, participation is restricted to taggers who live east of the Rocky Mountains.

Monarch Alert:

http://monarchalert.calpoly.edu/index.html

This program monitors the western population of monarch butterflies and is geared to taggers who live west of the Rocky Mountains.

Southwest Monarch Study:

www.swmonarchs.org/index.php

What if you live south of the Rocky Mountains? The Southwest Monarch Study recruits citizen scientists to tag monarchs mainly in Arizona, although it sometimes works with taggers in the Great Basin and Great Plains states.

Monarch Larval Monitoring Project:

www.mlmp.org

This citizen science project is helping monarch biologists better understand monarch caterpillar populations. Participants throughout the United States and Canada undertake a weekly survey of local milkweed habitat, recording and reporting the number of monarch eggs, caterpillars, and pupae they see. The Web site has everything you need to get started.

North American Butterfly Association:

www.naba.org

If you'd like to take your butterflying beyond the monarch, this Web site will get you started. NABA sponsors butterfly census projects across the country, and their Web site gives families a place to keep track of butterflies they've spotted in the field.

BIRD RESOURCES

BOOKS

A Kid's First Book of Birdwatching, by Scott Weidensaul (Quintet, 1990)

National Audubon Society North American Birdfeeder Handbook: The Complete Guide to Feeding and Observing Birds, by Robert Burton (DK, 1995)

What's That Bird? Getting to Know the Birds Around You, Coast to Coast, by Joseph Choiniere and Claire Mowbray Golding (Storey, 2005)

FIELD GUIDES

National Audubon Society First Field Guide: Birds, by Scott Weidensaul (Scholastic, 1998)

*National Geographic Society Field Guide to the Birds of North America, fifth edition, by Jon L. Dunn and Jonathan Alderfer
   (National Geographic Society, 2006)

INTERNET RESOURCES

Christmas Bird Count:
www.audubon.org/Bird/cbc
Visit this Web site to find a CBC event near you and for information on how to contact the compiler who organizes the event.

Great Backyard Bird Count:
www.birdsource.org/gbbcapps
The Great Backyard Bird Count (GBBC), jointly sponsored by the Cornell Lab of Ornithology and the Audubon Society, is a great way to get started in bird-based citizen science. Bird counts can take place anywhere and anytime during the designated GBBC weekend, and the minimum count window can be as short as 15 minutes.

Project FeederWatch:
www.birds.cornell.edu/pfw
BirdSleuth:
www.birds.cornell.edu/birdsleuth
These are just two of a long list of exciting and accessible citizen science projects coordinated by the Cornell Lab of Ornithology and dedicated to better understanding bird life on our planet. Whether you live in an urban or a rural setting, can dedicate a lot of time or just a little, are an experienced birder or a beginner, there is a birding project here for you.

Local birding projects abound; talk to naturalists at your local Audubon sanctuary, or visit its Web site.

*Starred books are written for an adult audience, but younger citizen scientists will find them useful.

FROG RESOURCES

BOOKS

Amphibians & Reptiles of the United States and Canada, by Paul A. Kobasa (World Book, 2007)
Frogs, by Nic Bishop (Scholastic, 2008)
The Frog Scientist, by Pamela S. Turner and Andy Comins (Houghton Mifflin, 2009)

FIELD GUIDES

National Audubon Society First Field Guide: Amphibians, by Brian Cassie (Scholastic, 1999)
*The Frogs and Toads of North America: A Comprehensive Guide to Their Identification, Behavior, and Calls, by Lang Elliott, Carl Gerhardt, and Carlos Davidson (Houghton Mifflin, 2009)

INTERNET RESOURCES

FrogWatch:

www.aza.org/frogwatch

The FrogWatch program has been placed under the direction of the Association of Zoos & Aquariums. The Web site includes guidelines for getting involved in the program, as well as links to information on the frogs and toads that live in your part of the country.

Music of Nature:

www.musicofnature.org

By no means limited to frog calls, this Web site is a wonderland of animal sights and sounds. Don't miss it.

North American Amphibian Monitoring Program (NAAMP):

www.pwrc.usgs.gov/naamp

NAAMP participation is restricted to adults, since listeners must drive a five-mile calling survey route at various times throughout a season. The Web site is open to everyone, though, and it is the place to go for up-to-date information on what species have been recorded by the citizen scientists listening for frogs and toads in your area. Want to find out how many frog and toad calls you can recognize? Click the Frog Quiz link to go to this fun, interactive section of the site.

LADYBUG RESOURCES

BOOKS

Ladybugology, by Michael Elsohn Ross (Carolrhoda, 1997)

Ladybugs, by Sylvia A. Johnson and Yuko Sato (Lerner, 1983)

*The Strange Lives of Familiar Insects, by Edwin Way Teale (Dodd, Mead and Co, 1962). This is an old book, and so it's a bit out of date. Also, it is written for an adult audience. Still, the chapter called "The Life of the Ladybird Beetle" is worth reading—and while you're at it, read "The Life of the Monarch Butterfly" chapter, too!

FIELD GUIDES

*Ladybugs of Alberta: Finding the Spots and Connecting the Dots, by John Acorn (University of Alberta Press, 2007). This is the only widely available, comprehensive ladybug field guide. Although it is about the ladybugs found in Alberta, Canada, the species described are fairly widespread, making it useful across North America.

*National Wildlife Federation Field Guide to Insects and Spiders of North America, by Arthur V. Evans (Sterling, 2007). Like most general insect field guides, this one dedicates only a handful of pages to ladybugs... but it's a start!

INTERNET RESOURCES

Lost Ladybug Project:
www.lostladybug.org
This Web site has all the information you need to get started in your ladybug work, including a field guide to common ladybug species, tips for spotting and photographing ladybugs in the field, a place to upload your images, and access to all 2,000+ pictures that have been contributed to the project so far.

BugGuide:
www.bugguide.net
This is the place to go when you've found an insect—any insect—you can't identify.

*Starred books are written for an adult audience, but younger citizen scientists will find them useful.

STILL MORE RESOURCES

MORE BOOKS

The Kids' Guide to Nature Adventures: 80 Great Activities for Exploring the Outdoors, by Joe Rhatigan (Lark Books, 2003)

The Nature Connection: An Outdoor Workbook for Kids, Families, and Classrooms, by Clare Walker Leslie (Storey Publishing, 2010)

MORE FIELD GUIDES

The guides listed on the previous pages are general in nature and, for the most part, describe the animal species found in North America. For a more specific look at the animals that are common in your geographic area, look for regional field guides at your library, local nature center, or bookstore.

MORE ONLINE RESOURCES

If butterflies, birds, frogs, or ladybugs aren't your thing, don't despair. Chances are there is a citizen science project that delves into whatever topics you *are* interested in. There are animal projects (Firefly Watch), plant projects (Project Budburst), and fungi projects (Mushroom Observer); there are land projects (Great Sunflower Project), sea projects (Global Dive Log), and air projects (Mountain Watch). There are zany projects (Project Roadkill), out-of-this-world projects (Great Worldwide Star Count), and earth-shaking projects (Did You Feel It?). You can study worms (Great Lakes Worm Watch), crickets (New York City Cricket Crawl), or the movement of money around the planet (US Currency Tracking Project). You can learn more about all these projects online by searching for the terms in parentheses, or you can visit the Web sites listed below to look for even more citizen science ideas.

Citizen Science Central:
www.birds.cornell.edu/citscitoolkit/projects

SciStarter (formerly Science for Citizens):
http://scistarter.com

QUICK QUIZ ANSWERS

 **BUTTERFLIES:**

A) Viceroy
(*Basilarchia archippus*)

B) Great spangled fritillary
(*Speyeria cybele*)

C) Monarch
(*Danaus plexippus*; male)

D) Queen
(*Danaus gilippus*)

 BIRDS:

A) Black-capped chickadee
(*Parus atricapillus*)

B) Hooded merganser
(*Lophodytes cucullatus*)

C) Mourning dove
(*Zenaida macroura*)

D) Downy woodpecker
(*Picoides pubescens*)

FROGS:

A) Wood frog
(*Rana sylvatica*)

B) Spring peeper
(*Pseudacris crucifer*)

C) Pickerel frog
(*Rana palustris*)

D) American bullfrog
(*Rana catesbeiana*)

LADYBUGS:

A) Multicolored Asian ladybug
(*Harmonia axyridis*)

B) Multicolored Asian ladybug
(*Harmonia axyridis*)

C) Three-banded ladybug
(*Coccinella trifasciata*)

D) Seven-spotted ladybug
(*Coccinella septempunctata*)

BIBLIOGRAPHY

Alderfer, Jonathan, and Jon L. Dunn. *National Geographic Birding Essentials. All the Tools, Techniques, and Tips You Need to Begin and Become a Better Birder.* Washington, DC: National Geographic Society, 2007.

Chapman, Frank M. "A Christmas Bird-Census." *Bird-Lore* 2 (1900), page 192.

Halpern, Sue. *Four Wings and a Prayer: Caught in the Mystery of the Monarch Butterfly.* New York: Vintage, 2001.

Harmon, J. P., E. Stephens, and J. Losey. "The Decline of Native Coccinellids (Coleoptera: Coccinellidae) in the United States and Canada." In *Beetle Conservation.* Dordrecht, The Netherlands: Springer, 2007.

Inkley, Douglas B. *Final Report Assessment of Utility of Frog Watch USA Data, 1998–2005.* Washington, DC: U.S. Geological Survey, 2006.

Losey, John E., Jordan E. Perlman, and E. Richard Hoebeke. "Citizen Scientist Rediscovers Rare Nine-Spotted Lady Beetle, *Coccinella novemnotata*, in Eastern North America." *Journal of Insect Conservation* 11 (2007), pages 415–417.

Mendelson, Joseph R., III, et al. "Confronting Amphibian Declines and Extinctions." *Science* 313 (2006), page 48.

National Geographic Society Field Guide to the Birds of North America, 2nd edition. Washington, DC: National Geographic Society, 1987.

Pyle, Robert Michael. *Chasing Monarchs: Migrating with the Butterflies of Passage.* New York: Mariner Books, 1999.

Souder, William. *A Plague of Frogs: The Horrifying True Story.* New York: Hyperion, 2000.

Stephens, Erin J., and John E. Losey. "The Decline of C-9—New York's State Insect." *Wings* 26(2) (2003): pages 8–12.

Thompson, Bill, III. *Identify Yourself: The 50 Most Common Birding Identification Challenges.* New York: Houghton Mifflin, 2005.

Urquhart, F. A. "Found at Last: The Monarch's Winter Home." *National Geographic* 15(2) (1976), pages 160–173.

GLOSSARY

Abdomen. Hindmost segment of an insect's body.

Antennae (singular: antenna). Sensory appendages found on the head of most insects.

Army. Term used to describe a large gathering of frogs and/or toads.

Beating stick. A wooden pole or stick used to tap or shake branches and bushes in order to dislodge insects for closer study.

Beating tray. A tray, usually made from a light-colored fabric, used to catch the insects dislodged from trees and shrubs by the beating stick.

Breeding generation. A generation of organisms, in this case monarch butterflies, whose collective priority is to reproduce.

Calling window. A defined period of time, usually several minutes, during which frog calls are recorded.

Census. A count or tally, especially of a certain population.

Chrysalis (also chrysalid). Pupal stage of the butterfly life cycle.

Citizen. Any resident of a society.

Citizen science. Study of the natural world undertaken by nonscientists; citizen science projects are often overseen by professional scientists.

Citizen scientist. Any man, woman, or child who practices citizen science.

Compiler. One who compiles, or tallies, the results of a census.

Count circle. A selected geographic area in which an individual Christmas Bird Count event is conducted.

Discal cell. The large, mitten-shaped orange area on the hind wing of a monarch butterfly or comparable areas on other winged insects; citizen scientists involved in monarch tagging programs affix a tag to the discal cell.

Dorsolateral folds. Symmetrical, raised ridges running lengthwise along the back of some frogs and toads; can be helpful in species identification.

Entomology. The study of insects.

Elytra (singular: elytron). Hardened front wings of ladybugs (and other beetles), which protect the softer hind wings when the beetle is not in flight.

Instar. Period of an insect life cycle between molting events.

Match hunt. A competitive hunting event common in the late 19th century during which teams of hunters raced to kill the most animals.

Migrating generation. A generation of organisms, in this case monarch butterflies, whose collective priority is a seasonal migration.

Molt. To cast off or shed feathers or skin as part of the growth process; caterpillars, ladybugs, and many other insects molt.

Myriads. Large quantities.

Ornithologist. A scientist who studies birds.

Oyamel fir. A species of fir tree (*Abies religiosa*) found in the mountains of Mexico and upon which monarch butterflies tend to roost in winter.

Proboscis. Mouthpart of a butterfly; used to drink nectar and water.

Pronotum. Protective body plate often mistaken for the head of a ladybug; the markings on the pronotum are very useful in identifying ladybug species.

Pupa (plural: pupae). Life stage of an insect during which the larval form—the caterpillar, in the case of butterflies—is transformed into the adult form; in butterflies, the pupa is also called a chrysalis.

Pupate. To enter the pupal life stage, during which the larval form of an insect assumes its adult form.

Range. Geographical area in which an organism passes its life; some organisms, like birds and monarch butterflies, have seasonal ranges.

Raspberry. A slang term to describe the spitting noise made with tongue and lips.

Scales. Specialized cellular outgrowths layered on the wings of most butterfly species; scales give the wings their colors and patterns.

Scent pouches. Pockets found on the hind wings of certain butterfly species, including the monarch; scent pouches may produce chemicals important for butterfly defense and/or mating.

Science. A methodical and systematic investigation of the natural world.

Spotting scope. A portable telescope often used by serious birdwatchers that can magnify objects 20 to 60 times; handheld binoculars magnify objects only 8 to 10 times.

Suet cake. Fat, nut- and seed-based food product made for attracting birds and other wildlife.

Survey. A study that collects data from wide-ranging sources.

Sweep net. A net used to collect insects from grasses, flowers, and shrubs.

Tympanum. Hearing organ of frogs and toads.

Vernal pools. Temporary, seasonal bodies of water that lack fish and are, therefore, important breeding habitats for amphibians and other organisms.

INDEx

(Page references in *italic* refer to images.)

ACKNOWLEDGMENTS

What a joy it has been to spend days and nights in the wilds of New England and beyond with my kids, my extended family, my neighbors, new friends, and whoever else was willing and able to explore with me. Every outing I took in relation to this book brought some germ of wonder that made its way onto these pages, and I am profoundly grateful to the gallant explorers who shared their company, their knowledge, and their enthusiasm: Cindy Dunn, Lisa Mattson, Kristin Steinmetz, the Streb family, David Krauss, Sarah Elliott, Peter Alden, Dick and Lucas Hale, Howard Sheinheit, John Liller, Kim Kastler, all the birders in the after-school program at Major Edwards Elementary School, Victoria Cormier, Stephanie Lussier, Stanley Selkow, Rick Quimby, Lou Perrotti, Kris Corwin, Ms. Stoff and her sharp-eyed fourth-graders, Eric Denemark, Leslie Allee, Leo Stellwag, ladybug guru Rebecca Smyth, and, of course, all the citizen scientists profiled in these pages.

Special thanks to Chip Taylor, John Losey, and Rick Bonney, who appreciate and encourage amateur scientists the world over and whose insights have influenced this project from the beginning. Naturalist Cindy Dunn taught me how to tag butterflies, advised my trip to Mexico, and was the very first person to read this book cover to cover; thank you, Cindy, for every single thing. Gracias a Gerardo que fue mi mano derecha en México, siempre te recordaré como un gran amigo que compartió tu cultura y bondad con nosotros.

Finally, sincerest thanks to Eric Luper, Liza Martz, Kate Messner, Linda Urban, and Ken Wright, the men and women who reminded me to come inside now and again to write, and to the gifted team at Henry Holt Books for Young Readers—especially Sally Doherty, Rebecca Hahn, and April Ward—who have championed this project with intensity, kindness, and savvy.